TINY HOUSES

THE COMPREHENSIVE GUIDE TO LIVING IN A TINY HOUSE WITH EXAMPLES AND IDEAS OF DESIGNS

© Copyright 2017

All rights Reserved. No part of this book may be reproduced in any form without permission in writing from the author. Reviewers may quote brief passages in reviews.

Disclaimer

No part of this publication may be reproduced or transmitted in any form or by any means, mechanical or electronic, including photocopying or recording, or by any information storage and retrieval system, or transmitted by email without permission in writing from the publisher.

While all attempts have been made to verify the information provided in this publication, neither the author nor the publisher assumes any responsibility for errors, omissions or contrary interpretations of the subject matter herein.

This book is for entertainment purposes only. The views expressed are those of the author alone, and should not be taken as expert instruction or commands. The reader is responsible for his or her own actions.

Adherence to all applicable laws and regulations, including international, federal, state and local laws governing professional licensing, business practices, advertising and all other aspects of doing business in the US, Canada, UK or any other jurisdiction is the sole responsibility of the purchaser or reader.

Neither the author nor the publisher assumes any responsibility or liability whatsoever on the behalf of the purchaser or reader of these materials. Any perceived slight of any individual or organization is purely unintentional.

Contents

INTRODUCTION 7

CHAPTER 1: TINY HOUSES AND THE TINY HOUSE MOVEMENT 10

WHAT IS THE TINY HOUSE MOVEMENT 10

Types of tiny houses 11

The joy of tiny house living 22

CHAPTER 2: DEBUNKING 7 MYTHS SURROUNDING TINY LIVING 27

Myth #1: Loss of privacy 27

Myth #2: Tiny house living is nomadic in nature 28

Myth #3: Goodbye modern conveniences, toys, and gadgets 29

Myth #4: Tiny house living is not for families 30

Myth #5: You need to be a handy person to live the tiny life 30

Myth #6: Tiny house living saves money 31

Myth #7: Living the easy life is a breeze 32

CHAPTER 3: FINANCING YOUR TINY HOUSE 33

Obtain a personal loan..........................33

Investigate a mortgage loan.................34

Acquire an RV loan.............................35

Make a cash purchase 36

CHAPTER 4: MEETING THE LEGAL REQUIREMENTS 37

Tiny houses as RVs 37

ADU Tiny houses 38

Making tiny house living a reality 40

CHAPTER 5: DESIGNING YOUR TINY HOUSE.. 43

Design and build your own home 43

Designing your tiny house...................44

Turning designs into plans...................46

Building your tiny house 47

Purchasing a tiny house......................48

Reduce your tiny home costs with these handy tips 49

CHAPTER 6: MOVING INTO YOUR TINY HOUSE.. 51

The Minimalist life - What to keep and what to let go.....................................52

Decluttering your life..........................53

Transitioning into tiny house living 59

CHAPTER 7: TINY HOUSE SPACE HACKS 63

Hack #1: Maximize your vertical space – AKA Pack vertical..................63

Hack #2: What can you hang?.............64

Hack #3: Layered Furniture 64

Hack #4: Embrace the outdoors 65

Hack #5: Create a hanging herb garden 65

Hack #6 Vacuum bags 66

Hack #7 Regularly declutter your home 66

Hack #8 Think carefully about what can come into your space 67

Hack #9 Zone your space 69

Hack #10 Mirror, mirror on the wall 69

Hack #11 Creative walls 70

Hack #12 Bookcases..........................70

Hack #13 White on White 71

Hack #14 Tiny Bath 71

Hack #15 Low Furniture 71

Hack #16 Ceiling shelves....................72

Hack #17 Foldable Spare Bed..............72

CONCLUSION **73**

Introduction

I want to thank you and commend you for downloading the book, "Tiny Houses: An Essential Guide to Living in a Tiny House with Examples and Ideas of Designs"

For those who participate in the tiny house life, a tiny house is a part of who you are, a mirror reflection of your personality, passions, and views on life. It becomes an extension of yourself. You are free to live the life that you want to live within the boundaries that you choose to abide in.

For many tiny house dwellers, tiny house living is a chance to go back to the essence of life. Some go off grid completely. They grow their own vegetables and use nature to provide their electricity and water. This is the life for the financially independent and free. No more mortgage bonds trapping you into a job that you loathe. With tiny house living, you are able to live within your means doing what you love to do.

As such, living in a tiny house allows you to be fully present in the now. You get to live a life free from clutter, chaos, and control. You are in charge of your life and what comes and goes.

I recently came across the following quote by Dale Carnegie:

People rarely succeed unless they have fun in what they are doing.

I love this quote. It embodies the purpose and heart behind tiny house living. Living in a tiny house combined with the heart of a minimalist is what allows people to live out the truth of who they are, to pursue their dreams and passions unapologetically, and to be present in the now.

Because tiny living has a way of keeping you focused on what really matters to you, your life becomes richer, fuller and more meaningful. While you may own fewer possessions, your relationships, and quality of life improve dramatically. One of the results of tiny house living is the emergence of a group of people succeeding in life because they are having fun doing what they love to do. This is how people thrive.

Out of this view and belief, this comprehensive guide on tiny houses was birthed. It is a means of teaching people what they need to get started in pursuing the life of tiny house living. A life where you can live fully. Leaving the past behind you to start a lifelong adventure of living the life you've always wanted to live but never knew you could.

As a result, you'll find in this book a taste of what tiny house living entails and looks like.

By reading this comprehensive guide to living in a tiny house, I hope to be able to help you with a starting point. From exploring tiny house living to the types of tiny houses available and getting ready to live in your own tiny house, we'll cover the essential areas.

I have also taken the time to weave into this book a list of some of my favorite bloggers, vloggers, and tiny house designs. I hope that by reading this book, you'll have a good grasp of what it looks like and means to live in a tiny house.

Without any further adieu, let's get started on our journey through the world of tiny houses:

Chapter 1: Tiny Houses and the Tiny House Movement

Tiny houses and tiny house living have joined a rising movement of living free and minimally. Why tiny houses when you can live in a house that is large enough to fit twenty people comfortably?

One word. Freedom. More and more people are becoming weary of a mundane routine in their lives that consists of most of their time being dedicated to a job they dislike for a paycheck that is mediocre. Am I being melodramatic? Perhaps.

However, the facts remain that the average American spends over 50% of their hard earned money towards paying off their mortgage. The vicious cycle doesn't end there. These same people end up living from paycheck to paycheck while they watch their dreams disappear in a puff of smoke. They have little time and money to devote to making their dreams a reality.

Until the tiny house movement was birthed.

What is the tiny house movement

Simply put, the tiny house movement consists of people throwing their hands up in the air out of exasperation and saying "No more. Life is too short to waste on a house. I have a life to live and I choose to live it fully."

These are the people who choose to downsize, getting rid of all their excess belongings and other goods that, let's face it, they don't really need. They are the ones who declutter not only their houses but also their lives. Their time doubles, their paycheck meets their needs and more. Suddenly, their dreams reappear with zeal as the realization that they can still live the life that they've always wanted and do the things they've always desired to do.

This is the tiny house movement. Living with only that which you need. People participating in the tiny house movement move from an average house of 2,600 square feet to one that ranges between 100 and 400 square feet.

TYPES OF TINY HOUSES

When it comes to tiny house living, your options for the perfect tiny house is quite vast. You can choose a home that fits the general standard of tiny houses or you could branch into the more creative tiny house styles.

To help you think through some of the design options for tiny houses, here are some common and creative house designs that you may like. Who knows, you may find the style that is perfect for you:

Yurts

Tiny house living meets camping when you opt for a yurt as a tiny house. These big round tent-like structures were the reliable, warm home for the Magnolian nomads. They can be dismantled in several hours and are a more semi-permanent tiny house than other styles. Plus, they are effective in keeping you warm during the cold winter months.

https://commons.wikimedia.org/wiki/File:Gurvger.jpg

Typically, a yurt consists of a portable wooden frame and a felt covering. The walls usually consist of a wood or bamboo latticework as a frame. For the floor, you'll have concrete that has been properly sealed and finished to support normal life.

Shipping container house

One of the more popular and mainstream tiny house designs is that of the shipping container. With shipping containers, your home is both fireproof and hurricane resistant.

Stick to the standard shipping container or have yours made out of traditional materials such as wood. Make your shipping container house your own by adding windows and doors for that burst of natural light.

Have a single container house for a simple and smaller option; or, combine several shipping containers together for a more average size house.

Prefab or modular houses

https://www.flickr.com/photos/designmilk/291101717
60

Get the house you want with very little effort by investing in a prefab house. These houses are built in a factory, brought to your location, and built within several days.

With prefab houses, you do not have to do much work other than choosing the style and focus of your house. Do you want it to be focused on aesthetics? Customize to your exact specifications? Do you want your tiny house to be eco-friendly?

Cob houses

Cob is a delightful mixture of clay, straw, and sand that can be used to build a tiny home. Both cheap and durable, cob houses are a great option for tiny house living for those who want to ensure that they stay "green". Fortunately, cob houses do not deteriorate drastically over time and this style of tiny house can last a lifetime.

https://commons.wikimedia.org/wiki/File:Home_at_Hollyhock.jpg

When it comes to building a cob house, the two main keys are to:

1. Have a strong stone foundation which will keep your walls dry and safe from rain, window, and other weather conditions.
2. Have an overhanging roof which lifts the direct moisture away from the exterior walls.

Vardos

Invest in the British Romani wagon for a classic, historical home known as the vardo. With this type of tiny house, you can create your own unique style or revisit the historical designs of intricate and colorful carvings and vibrant color schemes.

http://www.geograph.org.uk/photo/802765

Today, vardos keep their iconic design of a bow top and large wheels while their rounded ceiling allows the widest part of the wagon to feature the bed. Tow your vardo tiny house behind your automobile as you travel the country in Romani style.

Converted bus

A popular DIY tiny home project is that of buying an empty bus, removing all the seats and converting it into a long elegant home. Surprisingly, buses have more space than what we see; especially, after the seats have been removed. An empty bus gives you a blank canvas (so to speak) in which you are able to decorate and create a home to suit your style and preferences.

One of the added benefits of converting a bus into a tiny home is a number of windows and sunlight your home will have. You can darken your tiny home at any given time by adding curtains to all the available windows. Another option is to make the windows translucent so that you benefit from the natural sunlight while maintaining privacy.

For added space, you can design your seating arrangements with seats that lift up in order to incorporate more storage space in your tiny home. Another option for extra storage is to add trap door panels into the floor of your bus converted tiny home.

Trailer homes

Photo by Nicolás Boullosa:
https://www.flickr.com/photos/faircompanies/9044197514

Trailer homes are full tiny houses designed atop a trailer. Thus, they may sound similar to RVs but are a full mobile home. Trailer homes are among the more popular styles of tiny houses in today's tiny house movement. They are made mostly from timber and boast similar home features to your standard house since you can have a porch, side door, front door, windows, etc. The difference is that a trailer home permits you to move around with your home.

Houseboats

Some people find that tiny house living on land a bit too cumbersome thanks to all the legalities and other details surrounding tiny homes. Thus the houseboat became included in the types of tiny houses available to people. Live in a floating house, canal boat or a converted barge.

https://commons.wikimedia.org/wiki/File:LakeUnionHouseboat.jpg

With houseboats, you don't have to worry about moving it around the way you would a tiny house on wheels. You can keep it moored in the same location all year long if you choose. Alternatively, your houseboat could also be an alternative mode of transportation or a holiday home.

A-frames

With their slanted walls and unique architecture, A-frame cabins give your tiny home a unique geometric shape and rustic charm. Enjoy the steep slopes of the a-frame by turning them into bedroom lofts. Another added feature of the a-frame cabin is the large overhang roof giving you a covered porch.

https://commons.wikimedia.org/wiki/File:Traditional_thatched_house_(palheiro),_Santana,_Madeira,_Portugal.jpg

Turn your A-frame home into a two-floor tiny house by making use of the cabin's height and floating stairs. Not only will this help you maximize your space, your home will also feel more spacious.

Tree houses

Who doesn't like the whimsical and fantastical idea of living in a tree house? Not only can you relive the story of the Swiss Family Robinson, but you can also enjoy the resurfacing of those childhood memories you spent in your tree house.

https://www.flickr.com/photos/127478577@N02/1696 8477139

With a tree house, you can enjoy a permanent location while having the option to build multiple stories as well as several buildings.

As you can see from the above, the sky is the limit when it comes to designing and creating your tiny house. With a little bit of creativity, imagination and a lot of fun, you can have an affordable and dreamy home.

THE JOY OF TINY HOUSE LIVING

Remember the days when you were a child and you built your own tent or fort either in your bedroom, under the dining room table, out of your parents' sofa cushions, or in your backyard? Tiny house living brings back the exhilaration of defining your own space with the resources available to you. Building your own tiny house and living in it allows you the freedom to create a safe place in a large tumultuous world.

Freedom

As mentioned earlier one joy of tiny house living is the freedom it brings to you and your family. Where the typical house requires you to pay a hefty mortgage on a property that is permanent thus restricting your movements to the area that you bought in. With many tiny houses being mobile, you can change locations, travel, etc while taking your home with you. No need to sell and rebuy.

The financial freedom of tiny house living permits you to allocate your finances to that which you deem to be important. It may be saving up for your child's education, settling your outstanding debts or planning a way to fund a trip overseas. With your budget a bit more flexible, you can save your money for a rainy day, invest it, and more.

Declutter your home, life, and mind

With tiny house living comes the opportunity to significantly declutter your life, home, and mind. It seems to be a natural phenomenon to see our possessions increase in a bigger home. With more space available, we clutter our homes with unnecessary things. In a tiny house, you can only take with you the necessities. As a result, you take a closer look at what you really need versus what you want. Along with a decluttered house, you'll find your relationships and emotional well-being will follow suit. Tiny house living adds meaning to your life.

A decluttered lifestyle also ensures that your home stays tidier all the time. Goodbye piles of clothes left on the floor or on tabletops. In a tiny home, everything has its place and has to stay in its place.

Reduced time cleaning

Let's be honest, cleaning the standard American home is not only labor intensive but also time-consuming. With less square feet and minimal belongings, tiny houses are easier and quicker to clean. Living in a tiny house helps you to focus more of your time on those aspects of life that you find to be most important other than cleaning or dusting.

While we are discussing house cleaning, let's discuss décor. Home decor for a large house often requires careful planning and budgeting to decorate your home the way you prefer or as frequently as you like. Tiny houses allow you to decorate them for a fraction of the budget and you can even redecorate your tiny home all at once. On the other hand, a large house will be redecorated one room at a time.

Environment friendly

Today, the world is facing the growing reality of becoming more aware of the environment and the role that we play in keeping our environment protected. Tiny house living has quite a significant impact on the environment. People who chose to live in tiny houses have the option of living completely off grid thanks to solar panels.

Even if you don't go off grid, your tiny house will consume less water and electricity. All year round, your home will be cheaper to heat or cool since you are not needing to heat up a lot of space nor do you have all the rooms in your house lit up throughout the evening. You use what you need.

Tiny houses can also be made completely out of recycled or refurbished material.

Cost efficient

Besides reducing the initial cost of buying a home, tiny house living permits you to tailor make your home to your preferences, style, and personality for a limited budget. Some people may prefer contracting companies who specialize in tiny house designs and building while others may prefer to save their money and build their own home according to their unique design. Either way, your home will cost a fraction of the price of your standard house.

With a smaller square space to furnish, your furnishings and general running costs of your tiny home are going to also reduce drastically as will your utilities and electricity bills.

Overall costs of living and maintenance for tiny house living greatly reduce even with a few luxurious expenses.

The question now is this:

How much does a tiny house cost? What are the running costs of tiny house living?

Before we look more into financing your tiny home, we are going to debunk a few common misconceptions or myths pertaining to the tiny home living.

Chapter 2: Debunking 7 myths surrounding tiny living

Along with tiny house living, joys, and whimsical fantasies come a variety of myths. Some of these myths pertain to restrictions and an unrealistic surrendering to the supposed inevitability of giving up privacy, all that you hold dear, and a reduction in hosting guests. Fortunately, myths are misconceptions and preconceived ideas based on nothing less than an unproven hypothesis.

Let's get to debunking some of the more common myths surrounding tiny house living:

MYTH #1: LOSS OF PRIVACY

Many tiny homes make use of endless windows or large doors to create the illusion of space and to add light to their humble abode. This doesn't mean that your privacy is given up for the tiny lifestyle. Here are a few ways you can maintain a sense of privacy:

- Make use of window treatments, blinds, curtains or shades to give yourself that privacy.
- Investigate tiny house designs that incorporate walls, pocket doors, etc.
- Be sensitive to the privacy needs of others. You may find that you'll need to take turns getting dressed in the morning or being in the kitchen (if you have a partner or family member with you)

MYTH #2: TINY HOUSE LIVING IS NOMADIC IN NATURE

Is tiny house living equivalent to being a permanent nomad? No. Do you still have to move around? That depends on the state that you are living in. Your tiny house needs to comply with your area's zoning and building codes. If you are living in an RV Park then you may need to move around until you can find a more permanent location.

Of course, this is living legally. If your state accommodates permanent tiny house living, then you can set up a permanent lifestyle without having to do extensive traveling. If you join a tiny house community, you can also settle down permanently in your tiny home.

It all depends on how you choose to live and where you want to live. Of course, you can fly under the radar in the hopes that no one will discover you (that may be a bit more of a legal gray area so venture at your own risk).

I guess this myth is more of a gray area.

Myth #3: Goodbye modern conveniences, toys, and gadgets

I love toys and gadgets including the latest mobile phone or laptop. Not to mention headphones for my gaming times on the PC. And I admit that I love to be surrounded by beautiful things from art to soft rugs and elegant lamps.

You may think that tiny house living prevents you and me from enjoying these sort of luxuries. After all, we are talking about limited space here. That's the key limited space.

In a tiny house, you can have your favorite modern conveniences such as WIFI, TV, beautiful rugs, etc… All it takes is a bit of creativity and thoughtful planning. Of course, if you are self-employed, remote worker, or freelancer, you need access to the Internet, laptops, or PCs in order to do your job well.

Go ahead and buy your modern conveniences, just consider your budget and your space.

MYTH #4: TINY HOUSE LIVING IS NOT FOR FAMILIES

Whether you have a family or are single or newly married, you can live in a tiny house. The trick is to know how to plan your tiny house design accordingly and facilitate personal space.

Being single in the tiny house makes for an easier transition into the tiny house lifestyle. That being said, if you are a family, how about designing a bigger house (500 square feet) with separate areas and a porch. This way everyone has an opportunity to have their personal space and not be overly claustrophobic.

Tiny house living is not for those who are unable to live in very close proximity with other family members or whose negotiation and conflict resolution skills are poor.

MYTH #5: YOU NEED TO BE A HANDY PERSON TO LIVE THE TINY LIFE

I love today's era. With a press of a button, we have access to a myriad of information thanks to Google and

YouTube. In a lot of ways, we become a jack of all trades as we glean skills and information from the experiences of others.

The same pertains to learning how to handle DIY tasks and home maintenance. Tiny house living brings with it the opportunity to learn how to handle things yourself, be more independent and become more empowered.

MYTH #6: TINY HOUSE LIVING SAVES A TON OF MONEY

Saving money with tiny house living? Yes, to a certain extent. Your utilities and everyday costs do reduce some. It all depends on how you manage your finances.

The tiny house itself can be expensive or affordable depending on how you choose to finance it. It doesn't have to be expensive if you know what you want and how you want to fund it. For example, Melanie from the blog **A Small Life** found that she and her husband bought their Airstream home for $6,500 in comparison to the advertised price of $120,000 to build a TV tiny house.

Bottom line: tiny house living does save money but it is not a save money quick scheme.

MYTH #7: LIVING THE EASY LIFE IS A BREEZE

Whether you live in a tiny house or a standard home, life continues to ebb and flow with challenges, hardships, and joys. This is life no matter where you live. Tiny house living does help certain aspects such as less cleaning; however, you still need to prepare for those moments when you need to do some maintenance on your little house.

Chapter 3: Financing your Tiny House

Deciding that the tiny home lifestyle is for you is only one step in tiny house living. Even though tiny house living is a fraction of the cost of your standard living, you are still going to need to arrange finances to purchase your tiny house.

Fortunately, you can finance your tiny house with a number of options depending on your current situation.

OBTAIN A PERSONAL LOAN

When it comes to obtaining a personal loan, you have many options to explore. For instance, you could approach the bank for a personal loan, request a loan from your family and/or friends, or ask someone else that you know to loan you the money. You could approach people to sponsor your project through crowd funding platforms such as GoFundMe.com.

Whether you get a personal loan from the bank or someone you know, you'll need to work out a plan that will suffice for both you and the people loaning you the money necessary to build your tiny house. This usually will include interest rates ranging between 8 to 10% depending on the loan.

You can approach your local bank for an unsecured loan in which your bank will assess your credit history, income streams, assets and liabilities, current debts, etc. Should your bank find you reliable in managing your finances, they'll grant you a loan at a higher interest rate than other loans.

Unsecured loans have a higher interest rate because the lender is having to take higher risk. They have no collateral should the loan not be paid timely.

INVESTIGATE A MORTGAGE LOAN

Generally, getting a mortgage loan for your tiny house is going to be harder than expected since many banks do not consider tiny houses as houses. This is because tiny homes are often mobile and have a square footage below the minimum requirement for a standard house.

Of course, to get a mortgage loan, the banks will have to issue the same paperwork as if you were buying a typical home. In a nutshell, banks more than likely won't issue you a mortgage loan for your tiny house. Of course, you do get exceptions.

Another option to finance your tiny house is to use your current home as equity. This particular option is more applicable to those who already own a house. The key to a home equity loan is to already have settled a portion of your current home's mortgage so that you have capital to use.

For example, your current home may have a mortgage of $300,000 and you currently owe $100,000. You have $200,000 worth of equity which you could use towards financing your tiny house.

Acquire an RV loan

An easier option to fund your tiny home is to get an RV loan. For many people joining the tiny house movement, registering their tiny house as an RV is proving to be a more viable route in financing the building of their home.

The first step to getting an RV loan for your tiny house is to get it certified with the Recreation Vehicle Industry Association. Once you have this certification, you are then able to apply for your RV loan.

Make a cash purchase

Depending on your personal preference and financial goals, you can also finance your tiny home by making a cash purchase. This will entail a variety of options:

- Set aside a portion of your earnings until you have enough money to either purchase your tiny home in its entirety or fund it in stages
- Utilize your gifts and talents to make an extra income and use that money to fund your tiny home.
- Begin downsizing and selling on sites such as Craigslist. This extra money can be put towards financing your tiny home.

Chapter 4: Meeting the legal requirements

As with most things in life, we have to consider legalities and laws. The same goes for tiny house living. Although the tiny house movement is growing in popularity all over, especially in the US, housing legalities and minimal requirements remain a challenge.

If you are choosing to have a mobile tiny house, you are going to need to register your house as an RV within your state. If you are looking to build a tiny house with a foundation then your home is going to be registered as an accessory dwelling unit or ADU which brings with it a vast selection of complications. Perhaps this is why mobile tiny houses have become a more popular choice.

TINY HOUSES AS RVS

Registering your tiny home as an RV brings a lot of freedom to your lifestyle besides making it easier for you to finance. With your mobile tiny home, you can tour the country as much as you like while picking those places that you love to visit.

As a registered RV, your tiny home is able to be parked in your family or friends' backyard or driveway. Park your little house at an RV Park or camping ground for extended periods of time determined by each location. Of course, as an RV your tiny home won't be able to remain in one location indefinitely; however, the cost of renting a parking space at an RV park is considerably cheaper than buying a small piece of land for your tiny home to take up permanent residency.

The key with tiny houses as RVs is to take the time to have your home registered as an RV. You will also have to decide if you are prepared to either live a nomadic life or do extensive research on how to legally fly under the radar so that you are able to live in your tiny home for a longer period than a month.

ADU TINY HOUSES

Having your tiny house as a permanent residence is possible. Many tiny house dwellers enjoy the benefits that come with their home as a permanent spot on a larger piece of land.

To register your tiny house as a permanent home, you will need to find a piece of land that you either own or belongs to someone else who will give you permission to build your tiny house as an accessory dwelling unit (ADU).

Examples of ADUs include granny flats, garden cottages, auxiliary units, mother-in-law suites, etc.

ADUs do have to comply with the zoning and building codes of your area. Zoning refers to the area you are building in and the minimum size requirements. To find this out you'll need to ask your local zoning department.

Building codes refer to how you are to build your tiny home. This will be the minimum requirements of size and height.

In order to work with the zoning and building codes in your area, you may want to consider Ryan Mitchel's several possibilities:

- Research your county's laws, zoning and building codes in order to better understand the legal requirements in your area. You may also want to get a copy of the code book.

- Hire a contractor to help you cover all the legal and important areas of building a home such as terminology, utilities, sizes, and materials, etc. This may be an added cost; however, it will help to streamline the process since you are using someone who is an expert in building and who understands the legal requirements of your area.

- Work with your local code enforcement department. This may mean applying for an exception to the standard norms of house living. Submitting all relevant documentation and presenting your plans and goals to the department for approval.

Although, I am encouraging participation with the legal process of tiny house living, please be sure to do extensive research whether or not you live in a tiny house legally or illegally. The research will help you have a higher success rate in your pursuit of tiny house lifestyle.

MAKING TINY HOUSE LIVING A REALITY

Although tiny house living requires a lot of creativity to make it a possibility, many people have been able to work with the legalities to make it work. Here are a few tips from Megan Craig's post on Huffington Post that help make tiny house living a reality:

- Tiny holiday home - Use your tiny home as a holiday or vacation home. Living in a tiny house temporarily is more permissible in many states than a permanent dwelling.

- Temporary urbanism – This occurs when people take their mobile tiny homes to live semi-permanently on a piece of urban land waiting to be developed. Read Megan's post for an example of temporary urbanism.

- Tiny house community – Research the locations of the tiny house communities within your area or in other areas close to you. Living in a tiny house community will not only give you a sense of community but will also help you avoid having to work past the zoning and building code red tape.

- Change city – Find out which cities or states permit permanent tiny house dwelling. These areas will have more lenient zoning restriction.

- Be part of the law changing in your area – Petition your governing body to consider changing the laws in your area regarding tiny house living. Who knows you could go down in tiny house history as instrumental in advancing the tiny house movement.

Chapter 5: Designing your tiny house

Whether you are going to build your own tiny house or purchase a pre-designed home, you're going to need a design that encapsulates all that you want in your little mobile house. In this chapter, we are going to look at the two options you have at your fingertips namely:

1. Design your own home
2. Purchase a designed tiny house

A lot more focus is going to be on designing and building your own home since this is becoming more popular among tiny house dwellers. With the help of bloggers, vloggers, and hard work, you can benefit from the satisfaction of creating your own unique house.

DESIGN AND BUILD YOUR OWN HOME

I'm just going to come out and say it, I'm not a great DIY person; however, there is something fun and exhilarating about working at your own home. Brainstorming a variety of tiny house designs based on the research you can find on the Internet or via Tiny House TV shows is probably my favorite part of designing a home.

I love to pull out my pencils and play with all the various designs swimming in my head. I tweak here and there until finally, I have created a masterpiece. Then the hard work starts.

DESIGNING YOUR TINY HOUSE

When it comes to designing your tiny house, do your research. Visit a variety of tiny house resorts or hotels on your next vacation to get an idea of what you like and dislike about tiny house living. Get to know how you would do things when (if) you live in a tiny house. This will help you collect an array of ideas for your own tiny house design.

Simultaneously, watch YouTube videos such as:

- Living Big in a Tiny House which has almost 300,000 subscribers and an assortment of videos.
- Tiny House Giant Journey may have fewer subscribers but the videos are great resources.
- Tiny House Expedition is another growing YouTube channel on tiny house living

- Tiny r(E)volution which is focused on building tiny houses

Don't forget the Bloggers:
- **The Tiny Project**
- **Tiny House Talk**
- **The Tiny Life**
- **PAD Tiny Houses**
- **Tiny House Build**

For more popular tiny house bloggers **read here**.

And of course Tiny House TV Shows:
- Tiny House Builders
- Tiny House, Big Living
- Tiny House Nation
- Tiny House Hunters
- Tiny House World
- Tiny House Hunting

Finally, there is always good ole' Google and Pinterest for tiny house styles and design plans that are sure to inspire your imagination and creativity.

For free tiny house plans **go here**.

Turning Designs Into Plans

Once you have an idea of the aesthetical style of your house it's time to dig deeper into your design and how it will integrate into real life. To do this you'll need to ask yourself a few important questions such as:

- How much do you want to spend on your tiny house
- Are you willing to and capable of building your own home or will it be better to get someone to do the building for you?
- How big do you want your home to be?
- Are you going to build your home on wheels or have a tiny permanent house?

You are going to need to analyze your tiny home from every angle imaginable. Using your sketched design, work out the materials you are going to need, your budget and timeline. Decide where you are going to need to contract help and what aspects of your project you'll need to delegate to others.

Personally, I'd also think about the interior design of your tiny house so that you can get an idea of budgeting for your décor.

You'll need to price these out so that you know whether to save for the interior while you are building your tiny house or if you'll have enough in your budget to furnish your house on completion.

While you're at it, a trailer is going to be essential especially if you've chosen to go mobile (which is the norm among tiny house dwellers). Although you can get a used trailer, I highly recommend investing in a new trailer since it will ensure longevity and cost efficiency on the upkeep of your home.

The dimensions of your tiny home are going to either determine the size of your trailer or your trailer is going to determine the size of your home depending on what meets your preference and budget.

For more helpful information go to Sustainable Baby Steps.

Building your tiny house

Supposing that you have chosen to build your tiny house yourself, you're going to need to ensure that you have a large space to work whether it is on land or in a workspace as big as a warehouse. Of course, friendly neighbors would be an added bonus. Either way, you need enough space to work on your project and move it about.

Another important aspect is building equipment and power tools. If you don't have your own see if you can borrow someone else's or rent from a building store or local contractor.

With your power tools, materials, tiny house plans, and trailer, you are ready to go.

For a detailed step-by-step guide on building a tiny house **read here**. Tiny House Design also has a selection of tiny house plans for as low as $29 each.

Purchasing a tiny house

If you do not want to build your tiny house yourself, you do have alternative options such as contracting a contractor or tiny house company to build your tiny home for you. This will push the price of your tiny house up.

Another option is to explore prefab tiny homes. You can buy these homes already designed and ready-to-build-on location. Although they come in a more standard design, you'll be able to quickly erect your home with less hard work than designing and building your tiny home from scratch.

The method you choose to build your tiny home will come down to personal preference and capacity as well as budget, time frames, and design.

REDUCE YOUR TINY HOME COSTS WITH THESE HANDY TIPS

Whether you build your tiny house yourself, invest in a prefab house, or contract someone to build your tiny home, you can reduce your costs with these handy tips:

- Second-hand materials – See what second-hand materials you can find for your tiny home. With some TLC and patience, you can recycle a lot of products into creative hacks for storage or interior décor.

- Become best friends with sites like Craigslist – Do your homework and you'll be able to find an assortment of materials for free or at a significantly reduced price. Take your time to find the types of materials that you need and research sites such as Craigslist frequently. You could find yourself sinks, flooring, a dishwasher, vinyl siding, etc... for free if you are patient.

- Go shopping at second-hand stores – Window shop at the building second-hand stores in your city or area. This will give you an idea of bargains and what materials are available. With a little bit of shopping around, you'll be able to significantly reduce the costs of your building materials.

- Collect early – Leaving your shopping until the last minute won't help you save much money. Collect your materials early on in your planning so that when you are ready to build, you have all the materials that you need. This will also help you to get what you want at the price you want it for.

- Bargain – Bargain wherever you can. Learn to find quality products, appliances, and materials at a good rate. You don't have to settle for the first price that you get offered. Learn to negotiate and recognize a good deal.

Chapter 6: Moving into your tiny house

Now that you have decided on the tiny house living, the time has come for you to begin taking those small yet resounding steps towards the tiny house lifestyle. Let's face it, your tiny house is not going to arrive in your driveway or on your piece of land overnight. It's going to take the time to build whether you build it yourself or have a contractor do it for you.

While your tiny house is under construction, you can begin to prepare your family, lifestyle, and heart for the transition from a typical modern lifestyle to that of a minimalist living in a tiny house.

In this chapter, I want to look at what the minimalist life is (we already know that tiny house living is an expression of the minimalist life), ways to declutter your home and life and finally how to shop for your tiny house.

These are the essentials to successful tiny house living and are inseparable from each other. A minimalist requires that your life is decluttered which influences the way you shop.

THE MINIMALIST LIFE - WHAT TO KEEP AND WHAT TO LET GO

Minimalism is the process by which a person is able to ignore the clutter and noise of the world to live out their life's purpose and meaning. With society bombarding us with advert after advert and promotion after promotion, we find ourselves in a world where materialism and instant gratification are rife.

The problem with this is that we begin to measure our success and value of life against some imaginary standard that is beyond human reach. The result? A string of possessions that mean nothing to us in the grand scheme of things while we busily occupy ourselves with all sorts of activities and jobs that detract from what's really important in life.

Minimalism focuses on getting rid of the clutter, distractions, and noise of the world to find what is important to you (not to anyone else but you). It helps stop you and me from comparing ourselves to the people around us. We get to discover ourselves and live from that place of discovery.

Happiness comes from within not surroundings or belongings. As a child, I was taught this principle early on. My family lived a minimalist life although we didn't live the tiny house lifestyle. My parents were on a tight budget so we made do with what we had. At that time, they were missionaries in rural Mozambique so we had no TV, shopping centers, running water, or other luxuries. We lived simply and didn't complain. I remember often telling my parents that we were wealthy because we had a fun life and each other.

Tiny house living combines this minimalist living with a smaller home. The principle stays the same while the location changes. The journey towards minimalism starts internally. As you analyze your motives and reasons for buying and keeping the goods that you have, you'll become more aware of your internal motivators and reasoning. This leads to self-awareness. You'll be able to adapt your reasoning, beliefs, and habits accordingly.

DECLUTTERING YOUR LIFE

Regardless of the size of your home, big or tiny, clutter is a constant companion. Yes, it's true that the smaller your home, the less clutter you are likely to have. Still, your life and your tiny house need to be decluttered.

The biggest time of decluttering will occur when you go from living in the standard size home to your tiny house. Thereafter, you'll most likely experience moments where the declutter bug will bite and you'll be setting up a truckload of stuff to be donated, sold, or given to friends and family.

Fortunately, you can be well prepared with this list of tips and tricks (in no particular order):

#1 Start small

I don't know about you, but when it comes to decluttering my house I always want to do the whole house in one go. Turns out, this way of decluttering is not the most effective or encouraging. As stuff comes out of the cupboards and boxes upon boxes of goods pile at one side of the room, my heart sinks. All this mess in one room and I haven't even gotten to the rest of the house. Talk about overwhelming and discouraging.

A better way of decluttering your home is to start small. Choose a section of your home and allocate yourself 10-20 minutes to reorganize, sort out, and categorize.

Doing this a few days a week or a few weeks at a time will result in a decluttered home, life, and mind all while adding a spark of encouragement and accomplishment.

#2 Finish what you start

As tempting as it might be to start one thing and jump to the next, decluttering your home requires your focused attention and an ability to see each task through to the end. As you sort your things into categories of donating, sell, recycling, etc., be sure that you don't leave your things in the categorized boxes.

Organize to donate your donated items as soon as possible. If need be set up an appointment with the organization or shelter you are donating to, then do so. The same applies to all your other categories.

#3 Clothes, clothes, and more clothes

Love clothes, shoes, and jewelry? Me too. The reality is that we don't wear all the clothes, shoes, and jewelry that we own. We don't really need so much. Most of what we own lies in our cupboard longing to see a day of sunlight or social interaction. Alas, another day goes by and those clothes and shoes stay hidden in the cupboard.

No more! Go through your clothes, shoes, and jewelry. Find all the items that you haven't worn in the last six months. Put them aside in a box. (Side note: seasonal clothes should remain although you should also sort them out in this same process).

With your unused clothes out of your cupboard, see how you live in the next thirty days without these clothes. Do you miss them? Do you live blissfully unaware of their disappearance? If your answer to these questions is no and yes then you are good to donate your boxed clothes, jewelry, and shoes.

#4 Reduce Screens

How many mobiles, TVs, tablets, etc do you have in your home? How many do you really need? The answer to this question may differ per family. For example, an IT software developer who is self-employed may need two PCs with monitors to effectively do their work whereas a homeschooling mom will only need a tablet or a laptop.

For TVs, you probably only need to have one TV in your living room and not multiple TVs spread throughout your house.

While technology has its place, the amount of screen time spent in a day is rising exponentially. By cutting back a number of technological devices within your home, you are encouraging your family to focus on what is important – relationship!

Give your family and you the gift of family time and time outdoors.

#5 Don't rush out to buy unnecessary storage containers

I've done it before and you may have to. We decide to rush to the local store for more storage containers. This leads to an unnecessary purchase. Before you buy more storage containers, be sure to sort through your belongings first.

As you do this, you may find that those storage containers which are full are now available to store the things that really matter to you. This will save you money in the long run. Especially because you'll either buy that which you need or none at all. It ends up being a win-win situation.

#6 Emotional declutter

I'm putting emotional decluttering in this section because a lot of us have built up clutter in our minds. This clutter is unexpressed and suppressed emotions, dreams wants and desires, ideas and goals, to-do lists, and much more.

Journaling, creative work, or talking to someone you trust are all ways to stop yourself from being overly busy in life. By participating in some of these activities (or different ones) you'll be able to slow down and take stock of where you are at emotionally in your life. It's time to rekindle forgotten dreams, heal past hurts, and move on with the essence of you as you embark on the journey of tiny house living.

#7 It is a process

Decluttering your home and life is a process that you'll be doing for the remainder of your years. Yes, it will reduce drastically to fit in with your tiny house living. Still, you'll find that you'll be decluttering periodically throughout your life as you reassess what is necessary and what is excess. The beauty of a tiny house is that decluttering becomes part of a lifestyle since the small spaces force you to declutter the moment things start to accumulate beyond your space.

TRANSITIONING INTO TINY HOUSE LIVING

On the premise that you want to live the minimalist lifestyle and have begun decluttering both your house and your life, you are already well on your way to a successful life in your tiny home. Here are a few more tips towards helping you transition from the standard way of living to tiny house living:

#1 Assess your finances

Have a look at your budget and your current financial situation. What are the costs that you can begin cutting down on? Do you have any debt that needs to be taken care of speedily?

Considering finances are one of the biggest stressors in relationships and life, being in control of your money is imperative to a successful life. Find those areas that you can start making budget cuts while you work out the design of your tiny home, where you'll live, and how you'll build it (DIY or contractor or pre-fab).

#2 Need vs want

Most of us, if not all of us, struggle to discern our needs from our wants. Perhaps it's because we so easily can justify our spending. This is when we have, to be honest with ourselves. Do we really need that new pair of shoes or can we repair and redo our current pair? Do you want a blender or do you need a blender?

Another important question to ask yourself is how often will you use it? My partner loves coffee and I admit that we have a cappuccino machine, a filter coffee machine, a plunger, and a Nespresso coffee machine. The reality of these coffee machines is that we still drink instant coffee. We didn't need a coffee machine (other than a kettle), we wanted it. So, our next scheduled declutter day is going to see us getting rid of all the coffee machines that we don't need.

#3 Downsize

As you prepare for the tiny house lifestyle, realize that you may not be living in your tiny home tomorrow or next week. It will take time. As you wait and work towards the day when you do move into your tiny home, look for ways that you can begin downsizing.

You may choose to downsize your car or current living arrangements. Maybe you'll begin working through a room at a time, eliminating all the unnecessary goods that you won't be taking with you into your new season of life.

A fun way of downsizing is to go through your house a room at a time (don't do it all in one day) and put all your duplicates into a separate box. These you can then donate or sell since you will not have space or need for them in your tiny house living. (See the section on declutter for more tips)

#4 Journal your motivators

Journaling is a great tool for organization and insight into your innermost world. This is the place where your motivators lie. A popular way of vocalizing and realizing what is driving you towards the tiny house lifestyle is to write down all your reasons for choosing this lifestyle. Your reasons could be to be debt free, quit the job you hate, etc.

When the transition to tiny house living gets tough, you'll be able to read through your motivators to help you stick the course.

#5 Practice tiny house living

Next time you travel or want to go on vacation, pack only what you need to take with you. For example, three changes of clothes, one sweater, toiletries, etc. The goal is to pack as light as possible and see how you do.

Book yourself a stay in a tiny house hotel or resort. This will give you a taste of the realities and practicalities of tiny house living. You'll learn what it is you like and dislike or what you would do differently.

#6 Have a game plan

Now that you have a better idea of where you want to go towards your tiny house lifestyle, it's time to create a game plan. Carefully think about what your goals are. How are you going to go from living in a typical standard of living to the tiny house life?

For example, you may want to downsize first, pay off half your debt or more, and buy the materials you need for your tiny home piece by piece.

Whatever your plan is, make sure you have one and write it down. This will help you stay accountable and focused on your goals.

Chapter 7: Tiny House Space Hacks

Living in a tiny house is great. Fitting all your necessary belongings brings with it a few challenges and requires some creativity. After all, you only have so much space to fit your belongings.

This is why I put together a section on tiny house space hacks to help you maximize your space. Enjoy.

HACK #1: MAXIMIZE YOUR VERTICAL SPACE – AKA PACK VERTICAL

Perhaps the best space hack is that of stacking your belongings vertically. This is where I love my Tupperware and containers. Whether it is for food, clothes, or other belongings, containers can be used in any space while maximizing your storage capacity. I particularly love those containers or packing racks that have drawers.

See how much of your belongings and groceries can be stored vertically in containers instead of horizontally. You'll be amazed at how much you can actually keep with you in your tiny house.

Don't forget that you can also hang your containers on ceiling racks to further maximize your space.

Hack #2: What can you hang?

Regardless of the style of your tiny house, assess your space to see what you can hang and where. For example, you can hang your pots and pans on magnetic racks or strips in your kitchen. You can do the same for some of your cooking utensils.

Hang your everyday toiletries on a rack in your bath/shower. Invest in some wall-mounted pumps for your soaps in the kitchen area and bathroom. You may even want to include your shampoo in one of these pumps.

Those small hammocks usually found in boats can be used for hanging your fruit or other goodies up out of the way.

Get creative!

Hack #3: Layered Furniture

One of my favorite childhood memories was in our living room. Although I grew up in houses bigger than today's standard of tiny houses, my parents at one stage had a living room with sofas whose seats could lift up to reveal a gorgeous pantry underneath.

This, plus slide out drawers, is a must in any tiny house since they maximize space and keep your belongings out of sight. Ensure that you turn as much of your space into storage as possible. Your sofas can store belongings while still maintaining comfort. If your beds are not flush with the floor, invest in slide out drawers that could contain shoes, hobbies, toys, etc.

Perhaps you may wish to look into a sofa that can fold against the wall or into a sofa. Think carefully about how you can maintain comfort while making the most of your space and storage.

Hack #4: Embrace the outdoors

Where possible, embrace the outdoors. Spend as much of your time outside as possible. When the weather is permitting, cook outside, barbecue, work on your laptop (if you are a freelancer or remote worker), etc…

Hack #5: Create a hanging herb garden

Plants bring life and color into any home. Instead of a wreath on your door, hang your herb garden on your front door. Hang other plants on your porch or against the side walls of your home. This will add that extra homey touch with extra space.

Hack #6 Vacuum bags

For those items that you need to keep with you but won't use often, such as winter clothes or valuables that are a must keep, invest in vacuum bags. These bags will allow you to carry your precious belongings with you without compromising what little space you may have.

Hack #7 Regularly declutter your home

Regardless of whether you live in a 100 square foot house or a 600 square foot house, getting rid of those items that you don't use or need goes a long way to keeping your tiny house comfortable.

It's true that the less space we have, the fewer belongings we have. However, we do naturally accumulate things. Try to go through your house once every six months or so. Really analyze your belongings, asking yourself: Do I really need this? Will I use this?

The biggest obstacle to living a minimalist lifestyle is getting past that thought of what if I will need it someday. I have found that if I don't have something, I won't use it. Of course, there are exceptions to this such as a hand blender that blends, mixes, and whisks may be more viable than a bulky mixing machine. In this case, I'd give away or sell my mixing machine and buy the hand blender.

Regularly go through your clothes, belongings, utensils, etc., for those things that you are not using. See what you can let go and what you have to keep from a sentimental perspective.

If you are someone who is very sentimental, you can always take photos of those sentimental items (children's drawings, artwork, notes, etc) and store them on your computer.

Decluttering your home regularly gives you an opportunity to make some extra money from the items you can sell as well as being generous to the less fortunate by donating items that are in good condition and useful for charity shops or organizations.

HACK #8 THINK CAREFULLY ABOUT WHAT CAN COME INTO YOUR SPACE

It doesn't matter if you are out at the store or with friends and family, somewhere along the line you are going to want to come home with an item or two. This is the time to think carefully about what you want in your space.

Here are a few questions to help you:

- Will the item add value to your life?
- Will it add clutter to your house?
- Is this something you need or want? We easily blur the line between our wants and needs. Learning to discern between the two will help you keep healthy boundaries when it comes to keeping clutter at bay.
- Will the item work well with some of your other belongings?
- Can it replace another item and do a better job?
- Will it fit in your storage areas without taking too much space?

Often, we don't want to say no to people offering us a gift because we want to appreciate their heart of generosity and kindness. Yes, we do need to accept their gifts at times. Other times, we need to decline politely. It comes down to healthy boundaries with yourself and others.

Hack #9 Zone your space

Analyze your space. Think about how you can divide your tiny house into zones. For example, you'll need a section for your kitchen, a separate place for your dining room, a study and living room.

Plan your space carefully. What will work for you and where? Creating zones allows you to have designated areas to allow you to continue with your everyday activities.

Once you have your zones, you'll be able to strategically organize your storage accordingly.

Hack #10 Mirror, mirror on the wall

Whether I live in a small house or your typical sized house, I think I will always have my mirrors. I find that mirrors have this beautiful capacity to add light to a room while creating the illusion of more space. In a tiny house, this is even more applicable.

Use mirrors to emphasize the length of a room or to bounce light throughout your room. This will keep your home feeling light and spacious.

Hack #11 Creative walls

Think about the various ways you can create walls in your tiny house. You can use glass, curtains or floating walls to separate your rooms from each other. Glass allows you to create those divides but still emphasize the light in your home.

Curtains may be old-fashioned, yet, they are able to pull aside without taking up much room thus creating a wall when needed and more space when not in use.

Floating walls could be anything that you wish to use as a partition between the demarcated areas of your home. It could be a bookcase or a storage wall.

You could also use a sliding wall instead of a door to separate your rooms.

At the end of the day, your only limitation is your imagination.

Hack #12 Bookcases

Bookcases are handy since they can store more than just books. You could store anything in them really. Maximize your walls and doors by creating bookcases in one or two of them in your tiny house.

If you are going to create a bookcase on a wall, ensure that your bookcase goes from top to bottom and has a shelf for your TV, speakers and other necessary electronics. The remaining shelves could story DVDs, music, books, décor, plants, etc.

HACK #13 WHITE ON WHITE

If you enjoy white walls as a means of adding lightness to your tiny house, you may want to change your furniture to white. This will help you to create a feel of space and openness since white furniture will blend into the white walls causing a more spacious effect.

HACK #14 TINY BATH

Add stylish quirkiness to your bathroom with a small half size or three-quarter size bathtub. Now you can enjoy those bubble baths and your tiny house lifestyle all in one memorable experience.

HACK #15 LOW FURNITURE

When it comes to your furniture, low furniture works wonders to add that emphasis of height in your tiny house. For example, you could have an L-shaped sofa suite with throw cushions and drawers that slide out from below the seats. Because it's low, your space is broadened.

Hack #16 Ceiling Shelves

Combine low furniture with ceiling shelves to maximize your space and create depth and height to your tiny house. Store your books, picture frames, and other things that you don't need regularly up high and out of the way. Who would have thought tiny living would give you so much packing space!

Hack #17 Foldable Spare Bed

When I was in the hospital with my son a couple of years ago, the nurses showed me that some of the chairs they used for visitors could fold out into single beds for parents and other family members staying the night with patients. Later on, I saw the same concept but as an ottoman. Genius!

This got me thinking that tiny houses can have a spare bed without having a guest room. All you need is an ottoman bed – ottoman by day (to sit on) and bed by night (to sleep on).

Conclusion

Thank you again for downloading this book!

I hope this book was able to help you decide the type of tiny house that you would like to live in when you move into your tiny house. Or, maybe, you already have a tiny house and are wanting to make a few changes here and there. Either way, I hope that you've been able to find some helpful tips to add to your tiny house living.

I want to encourage you to keep on living the life of a minimalist in a tiny house. In a world where we have lost the essence of purpose and life, I hope that this book has inspired or confirmed the purpose for your life and what it is that you cherish in your life.

Whether you are starting your tiny house journey or continuing it, I encourage you to maintain a decluttered and simpler life. Use this book as a refresher or starting point. Continue to research and don't forget to check out the links in the book and in the references at the end of this book. These are the links that have helped me to compile this book and are blogs that I recommend.

Finally, don't forget to add your own flavor to your tiny house, your life, your relationships and your community.

If you have enjoyed this book, please be sure to leave a review and a comment to let us know how we are doing so we can continue to bring you quality ebooks.

Thank you and good luck!

CHECK OUT ANOTHER BOOK BY MATT BROWN

References

2015. Ethan. *16 Alternative to Tiny Houses.* The Tiny House. **http://www.thetinyhouse.net/alternatives-to-tiny-houses/**

9 Types of Tiny Homes. SalterSpiralStair. **https://www.salterspiralstair.com/blog/types-tiny-homes/**

2015. Rafter, Dan. *3 Ways to Finance a Tiny House.* Wise Bread. **http://www.wisebread.com/3-ways-to-finance-a-tiny-house**

2016. Shain, Susan. *Small house, big cost: How to finance a tiny house.* Selflender. **https://www.selflender.com/blog/how-finance-tiny-house.html**

2016. Nonko, Emily. *Tiny house zoning regulations: What you need to know.* Curbed. **http://www.curbed.com/2016/9/22/13002832/tiny-house-zoning-laws-regulations**

2011. Mitchell, Ryan. *How To Get Started: A Practical Guide Part 6.* The Tiny Life: Tiny Houses, Tiny Living. **http://thetinylife.com/tag/legal-zoning/**

2016. Go Banking Rates. *10 Loopholes to Build A Tiny Home Legally.* The Huffington Post. **http://www.huffingtonpost.com/gobanki**

ngrates/10-loopholes-to-build-a-t_b_9942198.html

2015. Gabriella. *Building on a Budget: The Incredible $8,000 Tiny House.* Tiny House Build. **https://tinyhousebuild.com/the-incredible-8000-tiny-house/**

2016. Melanie.*Ten Tiny House Myths.* A Small Life. **http://asmalllife.com/2016/02/11/tiny-house-myths/**

2016 Bastek, Tom. *5 Tiny House Problems Which Are Really Myths.*Tiny Home Builders. **https://www.tinyhomebuilders.com/blog/2016/04/21/five-biggest-tiny-living-myths/**

Four Tiny House Myths Debunked: Why You Should Still Consider a Small Space. Natural Papa. **http://naturalpapa.com/alternative-lifestyle-experiment/four-tiny-house-myths-debunked-still-consider-smaller-space/**

Hogan, Michelle Kennedy. *6 Great Ways to Organize Your Tiny Home*. Inhabitat. **http://inhabitat.com/6-ways-to-organize-your-tiny-home/**

2016. Lawson, Abby. *How to Get Organized When You Live in a Small House.* Just a Girl and Her Blog. **http://justagirlandherblog.com/how-to-**

get-organized-when-you-live-in-a-small-house/

30 Small Hacks That Will Instantly Maximize and Enlarge Your Space. Homeosthetics. **http://homesthetics.net/30-small-house-hacks-that-will-instantly-maximize-and-enlarge-your-space/**

19 Tiny House Hacks To Help You Maximize Your Space. Bidvine. **https://www.bidvine.com/articles/tiny-house-hacks-maximise-space/**

29 Sneaky Tips for Small Space Living, Listotic. **http://www.listotic.com/29-small-space-hacks/11/**

Millburn, Joshua Fields, and Nicodemus, Ryan. *What is Minimalism?* The Minimalists. **http://www.theminimalists.com/minimalism/**

2016. Becker, Joshua. *7 Ways toSample Living With Less.* Becoming Minimalist. **http://www.becomingminimalist.com/sample-living-with-less/**

2016. Beker, Joshua. *5 Life Giving Truths From Years of Living With Less.* Becoming Minimalist. **http://www.becomingminimalist.com/5-years-of-better/**

2014. Carver, Courtney. *7 Tiny Steps for the Beginner Minimalist.* Be More With Less. **http://bemorewithless.com/begin/**

2016. Morris, Catrin. *Pro-Organizer Tips: What Not to Do when Decluttering Your Home.* Apartment Therapy.
http://www.apartmenttherapy.com/pro-organizer-tips-what-not-to-do-when-decluttering-your-home-168836

Odom, Andrew. *How To Prepare for the tiny House Transition.* Sustainable Baby Steps.
http://www.sustainablebabysteps.com/tiny-house-transition.html

2015. Mitchell, Ryan. *Things That Will Happen to You Once You Move Into a Tiny House*. The Tiny Life: Tiny Houses, Tiny Living
http://thetinylife.com/things-that-will-happen-to-you-once-you-move-into-a-tiny-house/

2016. Becker, Joshua. *10 Creative Ways to Declutter Your Home.* Becoming Minimalist.
http://www.becomingminimalist.com/creative-ways-to-declutter/